SPECTRUM® READERS

UNIQUE!
Australian Animals

By Teresa Domnauer

 Carson-Dellosa Publishing

An imprint of Carson-Dellosa Publishing, LLC
P.O. Box 35665
Greensboro, NC 27425-5665

carsondellosa.com

Printed in the USA. All rights reserved.
ISBN 978-1-4838-0121-6

01-002141120

The continent of Australia has some of the world's most unique animals.
Animals that carry their babies in pouches live in Australia.
The world's only egg-laying mammals live in Australia, too.
Australia is an animal adventure!

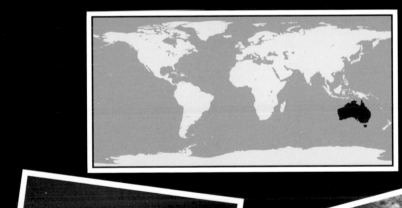

Koala

This Australian animal is a koala.
It is cute and furry, but it is not a bear.
It is a *marsupial,* an animal that carries
its young in a pouch.
Eucalyptus leaves are the only food
koalas eat.

Kangaroo

This Australian animal is a kangaroo.
Like koalas, kangaroos are marsupials.
They hop with powerful hind legs.
If kangaroos need to fight, they "box"
with their short arms.
They use their long tails for balance
and to signal danger.

Wallaby

This Australian animal is a wallaby.
Wallabies belong to the kangaroo
family and can jump very far.
The largest wallabies grow six feet tall.
That's about as tall as a man.
Wallabies will kick at their enemies

Tasmanian Devil

This Australian animal is a Tasmanian devil.
It is a meat-eating marsupial.
Tasmanian devils are only found on the island of Tasmania.
They growl, snarl, and bare their teeth.
At night, they hunt for birds, snakes, fish, and bugs.

Wombat

This Australian animal is a wombat.
Wombats use sharp claws to dig
burrows in forests and grasslands.
They eat grass, roots, and bark.
Baby wombats will climb inside their
mother's pouch to escape danger.

Dingo

This Australian animal is a dingo.
Sea travelers brought dingoes to
Australia over 3,000 years ago.
These wild dogs travel long distances
and hunt alone or in packs.
To communicate, dingoes howl
like wolves.

Kookaburra

This Australian animal is a
kookaburra.
Kookaburras are famous for their loud
calls, which sound like laughing.
They live in eucalyptus forests and
near people's homes.
They nest in tree holes and eat insects,
lizards, and worms.

Australian Pelican

This Australian animal is a pelican.
It has the largest bill of any bird.
Australian pelicans use their throat
pouches to catch and eat fish, but do
not store fish inside.
They live near water.

Platypus

This Australian animal is a platypus.
It looks like a mix of a duck, a beaver,
and an otter.
It is a *monotreme*, a mammal that lays
eggs and feeds milk to its babies.
There are only two monotremes in the
world, and both live in Australia!

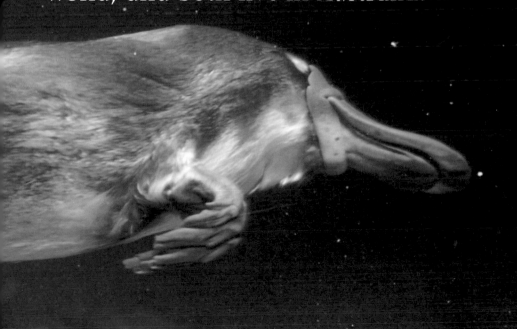

Australian Sea Lion

This Australian animal is a sea lion.
The Australian sea lion is the only seal
native to Australia.
It lives in large groups and dines on
lobsters, fish, and octopus.

Bottlenose Dolphin

This Australian animal is a bottlenose dolphin.

It lives in warm ocean waters.

Bottlenose dolphins swim in groups called *pods*.

These playful sea mammals squeak when they want to talk to each other.

Thorny Devil

This Australian animal is a thorny devil.

One of these lizards can eat 750 ants in a single day!

Sharp spikes protect its body.

Thorny devils can change color to hide in the Australian desert.

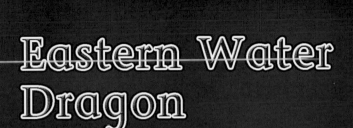

Eastern Water Dragon

This Australian animal is an eastern water dragon.

It lives in creeks, rivers, and lakes.

The water dragon can stay under water for 30 minutes.

This large lizard lounges in tree branches over water.

Australian Saltwater Crocodile

This Australian animal is a saltwater crocodile.
It is the largest reptile in the world.
A male can grow to 20 feet long.
That's longer than a big car!
Crocodiles kill prey with one snap of their powerful jaws.

UNIQUE! Australian Animals Comprehension Questions

1. How long can eastern water dragons stay under water?

2. How do Australian pelicans use their throat pouches?

3. Name two marsupials.

4. What keeps predators away from thorny devils?

5. What is the only kind of seal native to Australia?

6. What do Tasmanian devils eat?

7. What is a monotreme?

8. How do kangaroos fight?

9. How do Australian saltwater crocodiles kill their prey?

10. How do bottlenose dolphins communicate?